TAOISM

**ORIGINS • BELIEFS • PRACTICES
HOLY TEXTS • SACRED PLACES**

TAOISM

ORIGINS • BELIEFS • PRACTICES
HOLY TEXTS • SACRED PLACES

Jennifer Oldstone-Moore

OXFORD
UNIVERSITY PRESS

Oxford University Press

Oxford   New York
Auckland   Bangkok   Buenos Aires   Cape Town   Chennai
Dar es Salaam   Delhi   Hong Kong   Istanbul   Karachi   Kolkata
Kuala Lumpur   Madrid   Melbourne   Mexico City   Mumbai   Nairobi
São Paolo   Shanghai   Taipei   Tokyo   Toronto

First published in the United States of America in 2003 by
Oxford University Press, Inc.
198 Madison Avenue, New York, N.Y. 10016–4314
Oxford is a registered trademark of Oxford University Press

Conceived, created, and designed by
Duncan Baird Publishers, London, England

Library of Congress Cataloging-in-Publication Data is available

ISBN: 0-19-521933-3

Managing Editor: Christopher Westhorp
Project Editor: Diana Loxley
Design: Cobalt id
Picture Researcher: Julia Ruxton

Typeset in Garamond Three
Color reproduction by Scanhouse, Malaysia
Printed and bound in Singapore by Imago

NOTES
The abbreviations BCE and CE are used throughout this book:
BCE Before the Common Era (the equivalent of BC)
CE Common Era (the equivalent of AD)

Wade-Giles transliterations have generally been used throughout, with the
exception of some place names. For Pinyin equivalents please see page 106.

10 9 8 7 6 5 4 3 2 1

Page 2: A worshiper in a popular Taoist temple in Taipei. Religious
practices in such temples are highly localized and are generally performed
on an informal and individual basis rather than conforming to set rules.

CONTENTS

INTRODUCTION

The principal focus of Taoism is the Tao (meaning "Way," or "path"), which refers to a nameless, formless, all-pervasive power which brings all things into being and reverts them back into non-being in an eternal cycle. The tradition stresses the importance of following the way of the Tao—that is, of taking no action that is contrary to nature, and of finding one's place in the natural order of things. Understanding the pattern of the Tao includes the ability of trained specialists to control spiritual powers, which are either inferior to the Tao or emanations of it. Overall, the concept of the Tao provides a structure for making sense of the change of seasons, the life-cycle of creation, and the individual's place in the world.

Taoism has had a significant impact on the development of Chinese civilization and its ideas pervade virtually all aspects of the culture (see pp.97–103). Some of Taoism's most surprising contributions to Chinese and world civilization have been scientific. In the course of deciphering the pattern of the natural world in order to benefit humankind, a number of important discoveries were made. For example, the search for the "elixir of immortality" led not only to the invention of gunpowder (see p.100), but also to notable advances in Chinese medicine (see p.36 and pp.90–91). In the effort to align human life with cosmic energy, the magnetic compass was also devised—its first use was in *feng-shui*, the art of fixing the most auspicious site for buildings and structures.

Despite its influence on Chinese civilization, Taoism has been notoriously difficult to define—this is largely attributable to the many different and distinctive forms the tradition has adopted throughout its history (see pp.14–18). This historical complexity is partly due to the fact that Taoists have always been willing to absorb new ideas, personalities, and practices, including philosophical discourses, fresh revelations, the activities and techniques of shamans and makers of elixirs, and various deities. The schools of Taoism have never been united under a central authority, and the development of systematic teachings has not been an overriding concern, although

An early 18th-century jade statuette depicting Taoist deities being worshiped by pilgrims.

there is an organic unity in the various expressions of Taoism, particularly in the quest for longevity.

The Taoist contribution to Chinese religious practice and belief has been both overt and subtle. It is highly visible in some of the most important rituals, notably healing rites and funerals, and in techniques to attain immortality. However, in most other areas of religious practice its presence is less obvious. Chinese religion is an amalgam of the "Three Teachings" (Confucianism, Taoism, Buddhism) and the folk tradition. All three formal teachings provide methods for self-cultivation and transformation, but have different approaches which reflect concerns specific to each. Confucianism primarily addresses matters of government and social behavior. Buddhism provides an elaborate cosmology, a structured priesthood, and a detailed theory of the afterlife. Taoism meets other needs, and offers methods of spiritual and physical healing, a means of commerce with the spirit world, and securing blessings and protection. The popular tradition is typified by practices that vary by region; the worship, both locally and nationally, of hosts of deities; and by folk beliefs that cannot be categorized as coming from any of the formal traditions. Of the three major teachings, Taoism is the most closely linked to the popular tradition, but has remained distinct from it.

Relatively few people identify themselves as exclusively Taoist or Confucian, and there is considerable evidence to suggest that many members of the historic Confucian literati were also practitioners of Taoist arts. In the modern era, just as in the past, rather than professing a single doctrinal affiliation most Chinese people draw simultaneously from elements of all the teachings. Religious holidays reflect this syncretism—few of them can be identified as belonging specifically to any one tradition and most reveal influences from all the traditions. Taoist concerns and practices are clearly expressed in the quest for longevity and in sensitivity toward the seasonal patterns of change in nature.

Historically, Confucianism and Taoism have always served as foils for each other, and are examples of *yin-yang* complementarity in Chinese religion: the image of the worldly Confucian is contrasted with the Taoist recluse seeking an escape from human concerns; and the Confucian observance of the rules of etiquette is set against the Taoist's frequent flouting of social convention. Similar divisions were, and still are, often apparent within individuals: for example, a person may exhibit Confucian values in their professional life, but express Taoist qualities when retired or relaxing with friends—particular modes of being are chosen when considered most appropriate.

Despite the fact that Taoism is an essential element of East Asian culture, with an extensive literature and significant history, knowledge of Taoism has been, until recently, largely limited to a few philosophical texts. This is partly due to the nature of the Taoist canon itself—the abstruseness of many of the texts made them extremely difficult to decipher. As a rule, the canon was not studied by the Confucian élite who, for political reasons, were sometimes at odds with Taoist clergy. Additionally, very few copies of the canon were available until the twentieth century. Western scholars were also slow to begin serious study of Taoism, in comparison with Buddhism and Confucianism. Influenced by the biases of some prominent Chinese scholars, many of the first Western scholars of Chinese religion were missionaries who were appalled by the Taoist magical and exorcistic traditions. To their eyes, Taoism, as practiced by priests and people, seemed to be a debased and superstitious version of the lofty and philosophical tradition of antiquity. It was only in the latter half of the twentieth century that Taoism's complex, elaborate religious tradition began to be plumbed and appreciated—this process was assisted by recent archeological discoveries in tombs at Ma-wang-tui and Kuo-tien (Mawangdui and Guodian).

In addition to being a major component of Chinese society, Taoism also made an impact on Korean, Japanese, and Vietnamese civilizations, all of which were influenced by Chinese culture in the early centuries of the Common Era. Taoism's presence was relatively understated in these countries, and the tradition was integrated unobtrusively with local religious practices, especially nature cults, geomancy, divination, and shamanism. This influence became increasingly diffuse in later centuries. Many practices affiliated with Taoism, such as *t'ai-chi ch'üan*, *ch'i-kung*, acupuncture, and traditional Chinese medicine, continue to thrive, not only within East Asia, but outside the region as well.

The Taoist priesthood is strong in Taiwan, and Taoist communities have reappeared in mainland China in recent decades. Taoism has made inroads in the West too, where the availability of numerous translations of the *Tao Te Ching* have helped to boost its popularity and contributed to the establishment of a few nascent Taoist organizations and religious communities. There has also been a move to develop a Taoist-inspired ecology. Part of Taoism's appeal to Westerners undoubtedly lies in its naturalistic mysticism and in its concept of a universe in which humans and the natural world are integrated.

CHAPTER ONE

ORIGINS AND HISTORICAL DEVELOPMENT

Taoism has a complex history, established over several centuries. Traditionally, a distinction has been made between "philosophical" Taoism, identified as one of many strands of thought that arose during the Late Warring States Period (403–221BCE), and "religious" Taoism, which denotes a variety of religious movements, communities, scriptures, and practices, the first of which appeared at the end of the Han dynasty (206BCE–220CE).

The tradition has proved difficult to define because it draws on a wide range of apparently divergent ideas and practices. However, there is continuity between both the religious and philosophical traditions, particularly in the quest for longevity, the use of quiescence as a mode of being and cultivation, and identification of the Tao ("Way") as the source of all things.

LEFT:
A 17th-century Chinese painting depicting three Taoist deities, associated with long life, wealth and good fortune, studying a yin-yang banner.

Studies of Taoism usually begin with the figure of Lao-tzu (see pp.24–5) and his text, the *Tao Te Ching* (the *Classic of the Way and its Power*, also known as the *Lao-tzu*), traditionally dated to the sixth century BCE, but now thought to be a later text (see p.34). However, it is clear that the teachings contained in the text were developed in the context of ideas that were established well before the sixth century. These include divination, especially as articulated in the *I Ching* (*Book* or *Classic of Changes*); the theory of the complementary forces of *yin* and *yang*; the mutually engendering, mutually destroying "Five Phases" (see pp.64–5); and the notion of *ch'i*, the vital matter or life energy of which all things are made. Other early influences on the tradition included the shamans who commanded spirits, related ecstatic spirit journeys, and engaged in exercises that induced mysticism and deep, contemplative states. All these elements were key to the development of Taoism.

In addition to the *Tao Te Ching*, the classic works of philosophical Taoism are the *Chuang-tzu* (fourth century BCE), the *Huai-nan-tzu* (second century BCE), and the *Lieh-tzu* (ca. third to fourth century CE; see pp.34–5). These texts stress mysticism, the virtue of performing no action (*wu-wei*) that is contrary to nature, and learning and following the mysterious, constantly changing pattern of the cosmos, the Tao. There are also references in the first and last texts to meditative practices, to "perfected beings" who fly among the stars, to developing the capacity to "nourish life," to the limitations of human knowledge, and speculation concerning the relationship between the cosmos and humanity. Although each text is distinctive, commonality in subject matter created a loosely identifiable school of thought.

At the time of the first school of religious Taoism at the end of the Han dynasty, the spiritual landscape of China had developed in several important ways. By the third century BCE, individuals knowledgeable in techniques for achieving immortality—the *fang-shih*, or "gentlemen with recipes" (see pp.46–8)—were hired by imperial courts to reveal their secrets. By the beginning of the Common Era, Lao-tzu had been elevated to the status of a god, T'ai-shang Lao-chün, or Most High Lord Lao. The introduction of Buddhism to China brought the concepts of retribution and reincarnation, as well as an elaborate pantheon and a highly organized religious tradition. The chaos at the end of the Han saw a rise in millenarian and messianic hopes, some by groups claiming revelation from the deified Lao-tzu.

One such group, the Yellow Turbans, preached the coming of a golden age and emphasized therapeutic practices to increase one's lifespan and bring about spiritual purity. The Yellow Turbans rebelled in eastern China in 184CE, declaring the founding of a new state and a new era. The rebellion was quashed, but another group, the Way of the Celestial Masters, was established in Szechwan in the same year. The founder, Chang Tao-ling, established himself as Celestial Master, the head of a theocracy with an elaborately ordered hierarchy. Confession and repentance, including expiation of sin through public works, were offered as the means to healing and salvation (for one's ancestors as well as for oneself). In 215CE, the grandson of Chang Tao-ling relinquished authority to the new political order; in return, the school received royal patronage.

The Celestial Masters moved south in the beginning of the fourth century as political vicissitudes destabilized the north. There the school encountered another current of religious practice which focused on the achievement of longevity through medicinal, alchemical, and magical pursuits. The coming together of these two distinctive traditions, one with an elaborate communal structure, the other with a focus on individual perfection and salvation, resulted in a new Taoist sect, Shang-ch'ing (Highest Purity) Taoism. Based on Mount Mao, the movement was also known as the Mao Shan school.

Shang-ch'ing was initiated between 364 and 370CE by a series of revelations from a group of spirit beings from the Heaven of Highest Purity. The school emphasized interiorization and visual meditation, viewing the interior of the body as a microcosm of the universe. Scriptures were considered especially holy, and were carefully guarded from the uninitiated; Shang-ch'ing thus flourished among the élite. Another school of the south, Ling-pao (Numinous Jewel), drew from the Celestial Masters' practices, Shang-ch'ing's revelations, and the Mahayana Buddhist idea of universal salvation. The Ling-pao school elaborated and systematized liturgy and rituals—these are still practiced today.

The Ling-pao connection with Mahayana Buddhism reflects a larger trend at this time. The Period of Disunity (265–589CE) saw tremendous growth and popularity in Buddhism. Buddhists and Taoists vied for royal patronage with varied success. Both were changed as a result, most famously in the development of Ch'an (Zen) Buddhism, an amalgam of Taoist and Buddhist ideas.

Taoism enjoyed tremendous support during the T'ang dynasty (618–907CE). The imperial family shared Lao-tzu's surname, Li, and traced its lineage to him. The dynasty supported monasteries and temples, established Lao-tzu's birthday as a national holiday, and decreed that each family was to have a copy of the *Tao Te Ching*. It became compulsory reading in the civil service exams, which traditionally had used only Confucian texts. The Sung dynasty (960–1279CE) also traced its lineage to an important god of the Taoist pantheon. The Taoist canon was first printed in the twelfth century.

Of the many new schools that emerged in the Sung and Yüan (1279–1368CE) dynasties, two have remained active to this day—the Ch'üan-chen (Complete Perfection) and Cheng-i (Orthodox Unity), whose main temples are in Peking (Beijing). The Ch'üan-chen founder, Wang Che, supported a syncretic religion of the "Three Teachings" (Confucianism, Taoism, and Buddhism), and demanded the study of their respective classics. It was the first school to mandate celibacy for adepts. When Wang Che's disciple Ch'iu

A bronze statuette depicting Lao-tzu as an old man mounted on a buffalo, the animal that was said to have carried him out of China across the western border.

Ch'ang-ch'un was summoned to court by Genghis Khan to reveal the secrets of longevity, Ch'iu recommended sleeping apart from the imperial harem for one night, which would be "more beneficial than taking elixirs for 1,000 days." Ch'üan-chen emphasized interior alchemy (see p.90) as part of its method for internal purification. The Cheng-i (Orthodox Unity) was the restored Celestial Masters school. Unlike the celibate Ch'üan-chen practitioners, Cheng-i priests marry and pass on the lineage to their descendants. The patriarchs of this school are believed to be descendants of Chang Tao-ling. The 64th Celestial Master resides today in Taiwan.

In the twentieth century, Taoism suffered many setbacks. Religious freedom is guaranteed in the People's Republic, but "superstition" is to be eradicated—the practices of priests have sometimes been defined thus and suppressed. Considerable disruption took place during the Cultural Revolution (1966–1976), including the destruction of temples and texts. Today, Taoists operate under the auspices of the National Taoist Association, and there is some indication of renewed growth. The situation in Taiwan and some overseas communities is, however, quite different: the demand for the services of Taoist priests is great, and they are hired for festivals, funerals, and rituals at community temples.

Tao: The Origin of Creation

❝ There is a thing chaotic yet formed,

It was born before Heaven and Earth.

Silent.

Empty.

It is self-sufficient; it does not change.

It goes in all directions, but is not exhausted.

It could be considered the mother of all creation.

I do not know its name; I call it Tao.

If forced to name it, I would call it Great.

Being great, it fades away.

Fading away, it becomes distant.

Becoming distant, it reverses.

Therefore,

Tao is great.

Heaven is great.

Earth is great.

The king is great.

Within the boundaries of the land there are four great

things, and the king is one.

The person follows the pattern of earth.

Earth follows the pattern of Heaven.

Heaven follows the pattern of Tao.

And Tao follows the pattern of Nature. **❞**

From Lao-tzu's *Tao Te Ching*, Chapter 25, translated by Jennifer Oldstone-Moore.

Commentary

Much is disputed about the *Tao Te Ching*—its author-ship, dating, and meaning—but what is clear is that it has been foundational to the Taoist tradition, a source of great inspiration throughout history (see p.34). The text is about *Tao*, the "Way," and *Te*, "virtue" or "power," which is the activated power of Tao in man-ifest creation.

Taoists identify the origins of the cosmos as the Tao, a nameless, formless power and pattern which effort-lessly and spontaneously brings all things into being. After fruition, it reverts to its origins where the cycle begins again. The *Tao Te Ching* advises quiescence, and *wu-wei*, or taking no action that is contrary to nature. It also exalts the humble and lowly with the compelling image of water that always moves to the lowest place, and yet can wear away stone.

This chapter relates several of the Tao's key attributes: undifferentiated yet complete, formless and nameless, the source of all things, one with the movement and changes of Nature, eternal. The mystical oneness of the Tao is at the heart of the manifold practices and thoughts of the Taoist tradition, which themselves change and mutate into variety and color, but which nevertheless ultimately depend on the ineffable and colorless Origin.

福祿壽星君眾

御用監紀尚戚王勤筆本

令旗賽盛道

CHAPTER TWO

ASPECTS OF THE DIVINE

The divine manifests in a variety of ways in Taoism. In one sense, all creation is an expression of the divine, as all things come from the Tao ("Way"), and all eventually return to it. But Tao is not a supreme being, it is a cosmic principle, permeating and infusing all aspects of creation with vitality.

In seeming contradiction to this unity is the vast number of gods and deities who inhabit the cosmos. First there are divinities that are manifestations of primordial energy. Then there are gods of the created world: some are ancient deities adopted by Taoism, others are gods of the popular tradition, powerful figures promoted to the celestial bureaucracy after death. The contrast between the One and the many is appropriate: Tao is the cosmic principle that describes the unity behind myriad creation.

LEFT: This Ming dynasty (1454) hanging scroll depicts Fu-hsing, Lu-hsing, and Shou-hsing, three popular deities, who were associated with conferring happiness, high salaries, and longevity. Their attendant holds a parasol with banners aloft.

In Taoism, the source of the divine is the Tao. Originally meaning "road" or "way" in the texts of Chinese philosophy, in Taoism it becomes the cosmic principle that permeates and transcends all things. The Tao informs the pattern by which things become manifest, and is thus the Way of transformation and nature. It gives each creature its *te*, or distinctive power, once creation is brought forth. Formless, timeless, and limitless, the Tao, which begins as primordial chaos, gives rise to primordial or original *ch'i*, then *yin* and *yang*, then myriad creation. Tao generates and sustains all things in an eternal ebb and flow from chaos to form and back to elemental chaos.

The Tao is known in the human realm through gods and divinities who have manifested themselves throughout history. One of the most important is the deified Lao-tzu, T'ai-shang Lao-chün, Lord Lao Most High (see pp. 14–15). By the Han era, Lao-tzu was firmly established as a god; over time, he was considered coeval with primordial Tao from which he emerged prior to the formation of the universe. Scriptures describe a series of incarnations and metamorphoses during which he "waxed and waned with the seasons" before his miraculous conception by a virgin, eighty-one year gestation and birth through his mother's armpit. Lord Lao is the source of many Taoist revelations, including those in 142CE to Chang Tao-ling (see p.16).

There are descriptions and illustrations of Lord Lao's many incarnations, including his role as advisor to the sage kings of antiquity. In some texts, he is a messianic savior to the masses who will bring an era of great peace. According to the *Hua-hu ching* (*Scripture of the Conversion of the Barbarians,* written around 300CE), after Lao-tzu left China he continued his journey to India, where he became incarnate as the Buddha, seeking to bring the Way to those outside China. In the seventh century, Lao-tzu was canonized as the "Sovereign Ancestor of the Most High Mysterious Origin," and worship of him was officially mandated. Through example, scripture, revelation, and incarnation, Lao-tzu and his divine manifestations are key sources for understanding the Tao.

There are a number of other divinities that are emanations of the Tao; many are grouped in triads. They are from the remote heavens, pure and untouched by the created world. T'ai-i, the Supreme One, is understood cosmologically as the first stirring of the Tao, and also as a personified deity. As a deity, T'ai-i is a part of a triad, the Three Ones, which plays an important role in the microcosmic/macrocosmic scheme of Taoism, whereby all the gods of the cosmos are found in the body. The Three Ones reside not only in the cosmos but also in the three "cinnabar fields," or vital centers, of the body.

*A Ming dynasty shrine showing the Taoist god Chen-wu (top)
riding a mythical beast. The middle grotto is occupied by the
Three Pure Ones. At the bottom (center) sits the Jade Emperor.*

Moreover, they have come to refer to the three vital forces of the body: breath, essence (or semen), and spirit. In practices of internal alchemy, these forces are cultivated to create an "embryo of immortality," the foundation of an immortal body (see p.91).

Another important triad is the Three Pure Ones: the Heavenly Worthy of the Original Beginning, the Heavenly Worthy of the Numinous Jewel, and the Heavenly Worthy of Tao and Te, who is none other than Lao-tzu. The Three Pure Ones are rarely worshiped by the general populace; they are representations of the abstract power of the Tao. Instead of granting favors, they are invoked by Taoist priests in liturgies of cosmic renewal, such as the great *chiao* ritual (see p.59), bringing the creative energy of the Tao to renew community bonds.

Gods are understood and addressed as administrators and bureaucrats. The oral and ritual language used to address them follows the protocol of the Chinese imperial court. It was necessary to name and visualize these gods accurately, and an important part of training included revealing to the adept, in careful detail in documents called registers, how to do this. In visualization exercises, adepts work to establish and maintain the Three Ones in their bodies, thereby cultivating the vital forces to ensure longevity and immortality.

The Taoist pantheon includes many astral gods, and gods of natural formations, such as important rivers and sacred mountains. Gods who were popular before the development of religious Taoism were, over time, absorbed into an ever-growing Taoist pantheon. Examples include the Yellow Emperor (Huang-ti) and the Queen Mother of the West (Hsi Wang Mu). The Yellow Emperor is a ruler of antiquity, revered in the Confucian as well as Taoist tradition. He is considered to be an ideal ruler; the ancestor of all Chinese people, he was an adept in the arts of self-cultivation and longevity. One of Lord Lao's incarnations was as the Yellow Emperor's advisor, and together they signify the ideal relationship between ruler and advisor.

The Queen Mother of the West is referred to in the *Chuang-tzu* (see pp.34–5) as one who has "obtained the Tao," and is thus immortal. One of the most popular deities of the Han dynasty, she was worshiped by royalty and common folk alike. In 3BCE veneration of her inspired a millenarian movement in which large groups of people traveled west or waited in expectation of her imminent arrival to bring about a new age of peace and prosperity. She advised ancient rulers on leadership and self-cultivation and is particularly revered in Taoism for her techniques of immortality. (See also pp.30–31.)

Over the centuries, Taoism also absorbed the gods of the popular pantheon. These gods have human origins and gain their rank as gods when promoted to the celestial bureaucracy after death. At the apex of the celestial bureaucracy is the Jade Emperor. Sometimes identified as the younger brother of the Heavenly Worthy of the Original Beginning, he is the link between the pure Taoist heavens and the gods of the bureaucracies. He oversees the numerous gods of the popular tradition and is the celestial counterpart of the terrestrial emperor.

The gods of the popular tradition include a variety of personages, some of whom are widely worshiped today. Ma-tzu, for example, was officially recognized as a goddess after two centuries of popular veneration, and was promoted in the celestial hierarchy. Finally, in the seventeenth century, she became Empress of Heaven, a consort of the Jade Emperor. Another popular god, Kuan-ti, was a historical folk hero. He was known for his ferocity, courage, and unswerving loyalty to his blood brothers and to his king. He was captured and executed in 219CE—his story is told in the *Romance of the Three Kingdoms*, a famous novel from the Ming dynasty. Like Ma-tzu, his popular following grew until it gained imperial recognition, and he was granted titles by the emperor for his exemplary work as a god.

The Queen Mother of the West Visits Emperor Wu

66 The host of transcendents numbered several tens of
thousands. Their glow made the courtyard resplendent
all the way to the eaves. Once she had arrived, one did
not know their whereabouts, one only saw the Queen
Mother, riding a Purple Cloud sedan yoked to a nine-
colored striped dragon. Set apart on the side were fifty
heavenly transcendents ... The Queen Mother ascended
the royal audience hall, faced east and sat down. She
wore a full-length, lined, yellow damask gown. The
pattern and color of the gown were fresh and bright,
and her luminous bearing was pure and solemn. As her
belt she wore the Numinous Flying Great Sash. Slung
from her waist was the two-edged Image Separating
sword, and her hair was dressed with the Great Flower
hair knot. She wore on her head the headdress of the
Grand Perfected Dawn Infant; on her feet she wore
slippers with the Primal Gem Phoenix pattern. When
one looked at her, one could guess her age to be about
thirty; her height was perfect. Her heavenly demeanor
veiled the bright, lush carpet of flowers. Her visage
eclipsed the beauties of the age. She was truly a divine,
numinous personage. 99

From the *Han Wu-ti nei-chuan*, translated by Jennifer Oldstone-Moore.

Commentary

One of the most important goddesses, Hsi Wang Mu, the Queen Mother of the West (see p.28), is "the queen of immortals and a symbol of the highest *yin*." At her abode on sacred K'un-lun mountain grow various herbs and fruits that can promote longevity, including the famous peaches of immortality which ripen every 3,000 years and grant those fortunate enough to eat them 3,000 years of extended life. Legend has it that she visited the Han ruler Wu-ti in 110BCE on the seventh day of the seventh month, gracing him with immortality peaches, sacred texts, and powerful talismans—a story first told in the *Han Wu-ti nei-chuan* (*Inner Story of the Han Emperor Wu*), dating from the fourth or fifth century CE.

In early references, she is dangerous and wild—a human with dishevelled hair and tiger fangs. But she is later described as a beautiful goddess who greets suppli-cants with the splendor appropriate to a queen. Her youthfulness was attributed, in part, to her artful sexual practices. The Queen Mother of the West was sought out by adepts seeking immortality and a divine audience. Mount K'un-lun was understood to be a pivot between Heaven and Earth, a place visited by gods. Ascending this sacred mountain was considered to be both a literal and symbolic progression through immortality practices.

務成子

老君於夏禹時師務成子說開天經教以理化之道帝行之治滔滔之水鑿龍門導九河手足胝胵唘呱呱而泣三度過門不顧功成得天錫

CHAPTER THREE

SACRED TEXTS

The literature of Taoism includes a vast collection of works, from revelations, genealogies, and codes of conduct to sacred diagrams. The Taoist canon, currently in its 1445 edition, runs to 1,120 volumes. Few copies were to be seen outside of Taoist temples and monasteries until it became widely available after reprinting in 1926—and its unexplored depths are now the focus of considerable scholarly inquiry.

There are non-canonical texts too. Archives have yielded collections of scriptures, as have such archeological finds as the Tun-huang caves, which were sealed in the eleventh century and only reopened in 1900. Other works have been discovered inscribed on stone and bronze. Most Taoist scriptures are regarded as verbal articulations of the Tao, made accessible for moral, spiritual, and physical cultivation.

LEFT: An early 12th-century silk handscroll depicting the ninth of ten manifestations of Lao-tzu (see pp.24–5). In this incarnation, he appears as an imperial instructor, guiding the development of Chinese civilization.

At the heart of Taoism is the *Tao Te Ching* (the *Classic of the Way and its Power*). Tradition has it that these teachings were written in the sixth century BCE by Lao-tzu, a royal archivist. Disillusioned with court life, he set off for the western mountains mounted on an ox. At the Chinese frontier a guard asked him for his teachings—the result of this request was the *Tao Te Ching*, a brief text of just over 5,000 Chinese characters. It is written in mystical and allusive language, addresses the importance of taking no action contrary to nature (*wu-wei*); makes reference to methods and attitudes for preserving one's life; and gives examples of the Way of the sage ruler. Also known as the *Lao-tzu*, the text is now thought to be the work of several people and to date from the fourth century BCE; it is likely that Lao-tzu is a mythological figure.

The second great work of philosophical Taoism is the *Chuang-tzu*, named for its fourth-century BCE author, Chuang-tzu (Master Chuang), otherwise called Chuang Chou. His work is addressed to the private individual rather than to the ruler. Chuang-tzu delights in the infinite manifestations of the Tao and in its imperviousness to human values. He considers the nature of reality and reflects on the endless variations and transformations that occur in life and also in death, which he sees as a blending with the Tao. Chuang-tzu speaks of Immortals—perfected individuals who live on mountains, feed on the wind, sip the dew, and experience ecstatic flight. All these ideas became central to the tradition of religious Taoism. It is thought that Chuang-tzu wrote seven of the chapters; the other twenty-six were perhaps the work of his students.

Two other great works of philosophical Taoism are the second-century BCE *Huai-nan-tzu* (*Master of Huai-nan*) and the *Lieh-tzu* (ca. third to fourth century CE; and, like the *Chuang-tzu*, named after its author). The *Huai-nan-tzu* demonstrates how time, cosmos, and human action are mutually responsive and connected. The *Lieh-tzu* describes the Tao and its changes in a variety of stories indicating the marvels found in creation.

There are thousands of texts from the schools and practices that emerged in the Common Era. One of the most important was the *Pao-p'u tzu* (the *Master who Embraces Simplicity*) by Ko Hung, dated to 320CE. Ko Hung was a member of a southern aristocratic family connected with the Shang-ch'ing school. His text addresses the form of meditation of that time and the practice of alchemy; it shows influence from the *fang-shih*, or "gentlemen with recipes" (see pp.46–8), and the shamanistic tradition of south China. The *Pao-p'u tzu* is divided into "inner" (esoteric, Taoist) and "outer" (ethical, Confucian) chapters. The inner chapters relate secret methods and techniques for gaining immortality, including the creation of elixirs of immortality from mineral substances. The outer chapters are concerned with customs for ordering society and regulating human behavior. Morality, wisdom, and physical cultivation are all deemed central to the pursuit of immortality; one must be dedicated and faithful in practice, receive help from the gods, and have a skilled and trustworthy teacher.

These texts are included in the vast Taoist canon (*Tao-tsang*). The first attempt to collect and organize all Taoist works took place in the fifth century CE; periodically thereafter works were collected with new materials added to form new versions of the canon. With occasional proscriptions on Taoist material and the disruption to the Chinese heartland caused by foreign invaders and domestic rebels, early versions of the canon were destroyed, with some of the works lost entirely. Under the Mongol rulers of the Yüan dynasty, a version of the canon was produced with 7,000 chapters. Kubilai Khan later ordered all Taoist texts except the *Tao Te Ching* to be burnt after a dispute between Buddhists and Taoists.

The fifth-century canon was organized into three sections, the "Three Caverns," perhaps to echo the canon of Buddhism, which was growing rapidly in popularity at that time. The divisions reflect three Taoist revelatory traditions of the time: the Shang-ch'ing, Ling-pao, and San-huang (Three Sovereigns) schools. Other divisions, incorporating works of other schools, including those from the Celestial Masters, were added later. The Three Caverns are further subdivided by subject matter, which is wide ranging. One includes original revelations; another exegeses. Others are grouped around genealogy

A painting, from the Sui dynasty (581–618CE), of Taoist masters presenting the emperor with a new edition of the Tao Te Ching, *the central text of Taoism.*

and stories of the lives of Taoist luminaries. Charts, diagrams, and sacred talismans are organized; some sections have ethical prescriptions and sacred songs; and there are manuals for practices such as alchemy and geomancy.

Religious Taoism is a revealed religion. Its scriptures are emanations from the beginning of creation, formed by the primordial breath (*yüan ch'i*) that existed at the first stirring of the Tao. Thus the schools of religious Taoism, beginning with the Celestial Masters (see p.16), viewed scripture as the manifestation of the Tao on earth. The *Tao Te Ching* was understood to be a revelation by Lord Lao, the divinized Lao-tzu. He also revealed sacred registers of divine guardians—knowledge that enabled priests to summon and command gods. A famous recipient of revelations was Yang Hsi, who was visited by a number of Taoist spirits between 364 and 370 CE. The resulting scriptures were said to be from the uppermost heaven of all, that of the Highest Purity (Shang-ch'ing), and became the basis for the Shang-ch'ing school. The scriptures are highly literary in style, and Yang Hsi's elegant calligraphy lent them further prestige. Other texts, such as the *Classic of Great Peace* (*T'ai-p'ing ching*) of the Yellow Turbans (see pp.15–16), infused Taoism with messianic expectations whereby Lord Lao, or a representative, would usher in an era of peace, prosperity, and longevity.

Many Taoist texts are written in obscure or coded language to prevent information from falling into the hands of the uninitiated. Adepts were trained by masters who withheld complete teachings until they were convinced that the adepts were worthy to receive them. The final teaching would often be orally transmitted and was the key to the veiled and symbolic language that could only be understood by the fully initiated.

Hagiographies in the canon described the lives of Taoist worthies and Immortals and gave guidance on and examples of the path to transcendence. They also included the lives of divine transcendents, Taoist patriarchs, and a number of figures in local cults. Other texts related the teachings and writings of important figures in Taoist schools, such as Lü Tung-pin and Wang Che.

One unusual and important body of works in the canon charted sacred space. Many discussed the Five Sacred Mountains, including shrines and temples, and noted the Immortals or gods who have been seen or met there. A central assertion of Taoism is that the macrocosm is an exact parallel of the microcosm of the body. Thus, topographical texts contained maps of heaven, earth, and subterranean grottoes, important not only for traversing, making pilgrimages, and observing nature, but also for mapping the cosmos of one's own body.

A Passage from "Autumn Floods" in the *Chuang-tzu*

66 The god of the North Sea said, 'You can't discuss the ocean with a frog in a well—it is trapped by a confined space. You can't speak of ice to a summer insect—it is bound by one season. You can't speak of the Way with a biased scholar—he is limited by partiality. You have come out through the cliffs and banks and gazed at the great sea and know your relative insignificance; now it is possible to talk to you of the great underlying pattern.

Of all the waters under heaven, none is greater than the sea. The myriad streams return to it, the rivers ever flow into it, and yet it does not fill; it ever drains at the end of the world and yet it does not empty. Spring and autumn do not change it; flood and drought have no effect on it; it is immeasurably greater than the Yellow River and Yangtze.

Yet I never once took this greatness to make much of myself. I take my form from Heaven and Earth and receive vital breath from *yin* and *yang*. My place between Heaven and Earth is like that of a small stone or tree on a large mountain. I see that I am small—on what account would I regard myself as great?' 99

From the *Chuang-tzu*, translated by Jennifer Oldstone-Moore.

Commentary

The works of philosophical Taoism are cherished in the Chinese literary tradition for their mystical vision, arresting images, and outstanding literary beauty. This is especially true of the eponymous work of Chuang-tzu (ca. 369–286BCE), whose text is typified by fantastic conversations and playful yet profound and poignant observations.

Chuang-tzu affirms the eternal flux of nature, the ever-shifting shapes and manifestations of the natural world that are part of a glorious whole, where nothing is ever lost and from whose vantage point all things must be considered as being equally precious and significant. The central goal for humans is to learn the impartiality and all-encompassing nature of the Tao, and, like the Tao, to understand creation and experience from an ultimate perspective, rather than from a selfish and limited vantage point.

The featured passage from "Autumn Floods" demonstrates this idea. The river god had been boasting of his greatness, until he was humbled by his encounter with the vast sea. The god of the sea reflects on the necessarily limited perspective of any creature in the cosmos; he then embraces the philosophy of the Tao and observes that even the sea must be considered tiny in the great scheme of Heaven and Earth.

CHAPTER FOUR

SACRED PERSONS

The history of Taoism is filled with illustrious figures. Many famous Taoists—frequently those who experienced revelations from divinities—are founders of schools of Taoism. Such notables often received royal patronage and enjoyed prestige at court. Local priests were the most visible representatives of Taoism and were hired for healing, exorcisms, and rituals; their various powers inspired awe and fear.

Other Taoists, such as Lao-tzu and Chuang-tzu, are renowned for their rejection of society and worldly ambition. There are many stories of Immortals who have transcended both human and divine existence. Some Taoists, like the Seven Sages of the Bamboo Grove, revelled in their freedom from society's constraints, and spent their time appreciating nature and the virtues of wine and good conversation.

LEFT:
The Eight Immortals and the son of the Jade Emperor are represented on this large joss stick. Joss is made from the trunk of the cinnamon tree. Ground into powder, and mixed with sawdust and water, it is molded into shape, painted with symbolic colors, and then burned as an offering.

Taoist priests, ordained members of the clergy, are able to summon and command the multitude of beings that make up the spirit world. Such awesome power commands great respect. Through training and memorization of esoteric scriptures, they have the ability to call and direct supernatural forces, to confer benefits, and to fight demons. They are commonly employed as exorcists—for example, to appease earth spirits inhabiting the site of a planned new building, to remove ghosts, or to dispel demons who may be causing mental or physical distress.

A priest summons the spirits by making magical gestures and reciting chants and scriptures. Holy water and, sometimes, flaming alcohol are also used, either sprinkled or sprayed through the mouth over a written spell. Other ritual techniques include the "Dance of Yü," a dance patterned on the gait of the legendary ruler. This command of spirits enables Taoist priests to play key roles at funerals. As masters of the celestial and infernal bureaucracies of the world of spirits, they know how to compose writs of pardon and perform the rituals that will speed the soul through the afterlife.

Taoist clergy follow a variety of paths. Some withdraw from the community to live as hermits or monastics and practice self-cultivation, while others are "fire-dwellers" who marry and live with their families, performing rites of healing and exorcism in the community. Of the priests who work in the community, there is a distinction between the "blackheaded" and "redheaded" Taoists, referring to the distinctive headdress of each. Redheaded Taoists are, in effect, shamans who can access the local spirits and perform dramatic exorcisms. Blackheaded priests are orthodox: they are literate and have received extensive training. Rather than managing a mere handful of gods, they are able to control celestial hosts as well as to summon the divinities who are pure emanations of Tao. Contemporary fire-dwelling priests are from the (blackheaded) Orthodox Unity, or Cheng-i school and they claim lineage with the Celestial Masters of the Han dynasty. Their order is hereditary: sons learn rituals as they grow up, they are initiated into secret lore, and inherit family ceremonial robes and texts. It is the blackheaded priests who perform elaborate rituals of penitence and renewal such as the *chiao* (see p.59). Both blackheaded and redheaded priests may be hired at a community temple where they may perform their services side-by-side and in the company of other religious specialists.

Historically, those who became monastic Taoists were typically novices between the ages of twelve and 20 and began monastic life with menial labor, in addition to the daily practice of devotions. Some monasteries were open to Taoists of all schools, as well as to individuals who wished to pursue Taoist practices of self-cultivation. The Complete Perfection, or Ch'üan-chen, school is the main monastic school to have survived to the present day; it is unusual in that it is a celibate, vegetarian order.

Many famous Taoists cultivated connections at court. Beginning in 215CE with the ceding of power by Celestial Master Chang Lu to the ruler of the new Wei dynasty, Taoists have used political authority to enjoy the favor of temporal rulers and to grant a special legitimacy to their own teachings. Another Celestial Master, K'ou Ch'ien-chih (365–448CE) both reformed the Celestial Master school, ending sexual rites which had by this time become infamous, and convinced the emperor to prohibit Buddhism.

Several illustrious Taoists were advisors to emperors, such as Tu Kuang-t'ing (850–933CE), a Taoist scholar of the T'ang Court. Some rulers received religious titles from these high ranking Taoists, including Sung emperor Hui-tsung (r. 1101–1125CE), who set up a theocracy, placing himself at the apex of the Taoist pantheon. The Taoist as advisor and teacher to the emperor had antecedents in the *fang-shih*, the "gentlemen with

The Seven Sages of the Bamboo Grove *by Fu Pao-shih (1904–1965). This group of 3rd-century* CE *scholars rejected worldly ambition for a life in pursuit of the Tao.*

recipes" who flourished before the Common Era. The *fang-shih* were the emperor's official magicians and performed a wide range of functions, which were later continued in various forms by priests. These included communicating with ghosts and spirits, performing exorcisms, and practicing various types of divination. They also performed acupuncture and moxibustion, prescribed special regimes of hygiene, diet and medication, and techniques for sexual vitality.

Stories of Immortals date from Chinese antiquity. Taoist texts described their various forms and characteristics. There are accounts of Immortals who do not experience hunger or cold, who are able to pass through fire without burning and through water without getting wet, who have feathers and are as light as birds, and who transform their old bodies into young ones. Some ride dragons, cranes, or phoenixes. Masters of time and space, they are able to reduce the world to the size of a gourd or to turn a gourd into a world as vast as the universe. They are also evanescent, appearing and disappearing at will. Their flesh is as smooth as ice, they have snow-white skin, and strange features, such as square pupils and long ears. Immortals live in remote mountains and caves, or in magic places, such as P'eng-lai Island off the Chinese mainland. They walk among the stars and planets, occasionally visiting the earth incognito to grant immortality to deserving mortals.

Immortals occupy a unique place in the hierarchy of beings. They are humans who have realized the Tao and are free from the concerns of both humans and the gods, beyond the anxieties and distractions of either the terrestrial or celestial bureaucracies.

Many Chinese folk stories tell of the Eight Immortals—a group of "perfected persons" who attained immortality. They are a diverse group, associated with blessings and happiness and the "Eight Conditions of Life" (youth, age, poverty, wealth, high rank, common rank, femininity, and masculinity). Their varied experiences, status, and methods for immortality represent the accessibility of perfection to any who choose to pursue it.

One of the Eight Immortals, Lü Tung-pin, is credited with establishing the Complete Perfection school, and co-authoring texts on alchemy with his master Chung-li Ch'üan. Upon meeting Chung-li for the first time, Lü magically experienced an entire lifetime of worldly achievements and disasters in the few minutes it took him to prepare a pot of millet. Awakening to his meal and to the folly of mundane pursuits, he abandoned a conventional life to become an itinerant Taoist.

In literature and fable, Immortals and other Taoist heroes exemplify those who practice intense self-cultivation to absorb the teachings of Taoism in order to acquire magical powers and, above all, achieve immortality. Although admired, these figures are often unconventional. The ragged Taoist monk, free from society's bonds, laughing uproariously and irreverently, is a recurrent literary image.

"In Praise of the Virtues of Wine" by Liu Ling

❜ There is Mr Great Man:

He takes Heaven and Earth to be one day,

Ten thousand years to be one moment

The sun and moon are his windows;

The eight barren places are his palaces.

He travels without tracks or traces

He lives without room or cottage

Heaven is his curtain, the earth his mat

Self-indulgent, he does what he pleases...

No worries, no brooding,

He is content and well pleased.

He becomes intoxicated without moving;

All of a sudden, he awakens from his drunkenness...

He doesn't know the feeling of flesh hurt by bitter cold
or searing heat,

Or the sensations of covetousness

Gazing down, he watches the rest of the world
agitated and unsettled

    like bits of duckweed borne on the Yangtze and

    Han rivers... ❞

From Liu Ling's "Chiu-te sung," in the *Wen-hsüan*, translated by Jennifer Oldstone-Moore.

Commentary

The Seven Sages of the Bamboo Grove were a group of friends living in the third century CE during a time of dynastic collapse—a period of great anxiety and uncertainty. They eschewed the court and worldly ambition for a carefree and elegant life in pursuit of the Tao. Their lives combined erudition with highly unconventional behavior: one of the seven is said to have given up using cups—instead, he drank his wine from a communal bowl which was placed on the ground and sometimes shared by the family pigs.

Liu Ling, the author of this poem, "Chiu-te Sung" ("In Praise of the Virtues of Wine"), was famous for his uninhibited behavior and freedom from the rules and mores of polite society. Sometimes, having drunk much wine, he would take off his clothes and sit naked in his room. When criticized for doing this by one of his visitors, Liu responded, "The universe is my home; the room my trousers—what are you doing in my trousers?"

Liu's poem describes the existence of the Taoist who retreats from the world and views it with detached amusement. Down through the centuries, a disregard for the niceties of etiquette, together with a love of poetry, wine, and music, all became attributes of Taoist eccentrics and sages.

CHAPTER FIVE

ETHICAL PRINCIPLES

The ethics of the earliest texts of Taoism take the perspective of the Tao, which creates, nurtures, destroys, and embraces all things. Human conventions, which privilege human concerns and divide the world into opposites, such as good and bad, are not to be trusted, for they make following the pattern of the Tao impossible.

By the Common Era, more conventional ethical principles were added to the earlier ideals—all emphasized the pursuit of longevity. Distinctly Taoist ethics—such as flexibility, humility, embracing the feminine side, and, above all, taking no action contrary to nature (*wu-wei*)—were gradually and harmoniously combined with ethical principles drawn from the varied traditions of other Chinese religions, in particular, from Confucianism and Buddhism.

*LEFT:
Charms on a souvenir stall at the entrance to the Temple of Wong Tai Sin in Kowloon, Hong Kong. Wong Tai Sin is a local deity renowned for the accuracy of his predictions. These charms are worn as jewelry or placed in the home to bring good luck.*

A striking passage from the *Tao Te Ching* states that neither Heaven and Earth nor the sage are benevolent. Heaven and Earth treat all things as "straw dogs," as implements to be discarded after they are used; the sage treats the people in the same way. This rather startling doctrine of non-preference, and of taking the priorities of nature rather than society, informs the ethics of the earliest Taoist writings. According to this worldview, conventional morality—which is based on distinctions between good and bad, beauty and ugliness, value and worthlessness—is dangerous as well as irrelevant. It is only when people become aware of distinctions between things that they learn to covet and desire; any statements advocating a specific virtue, such as beauty or goodness, will imply and even create its opposite.

At the core of the ethics of philosophical Taoism is *wu-wei*, or "noninterference," which demands that one submit to and move with, rather than against, natural processes and change. Just as the Tao shows no favorites among creatures, the sage human privileges no particular mode or outcome, but rather follows this pattern itself, gaining the power of the force of nature.

The rejection of conventional modes is demonstrated in the story of Hun-tun, the cosmic gourd. The gourd, a favorite symbol of Taoists, is a lumpy and irregularly shaped container of seeds that symbolizes the creative potential of undifferentiated Tao. In the story, the cosmic gourd Hun-tun is the king of the center, who naturally and generously bestows gifts on the kings of the north and south. These kings do not react spontaneously, but fret about proper protocol in gift-giving. Their response is to bore seven holes into Hun-tun, to provide him with human orifices and thus give him the prestige of a human face. But when they have finished their drilling, he dies. The story illustrates the dangers of assuming human-oriented bias, and the ideal of natural and spontaneous action which existed in the Taoist golden age, before the advent of the destructive and perverting rules and protocols of civilization.

Return to the boundless potential and undifferentiated perfection of the primal state continued to be the goal in religious Taoism and the quest for immortality. By the Common Era, however, the prescriptions of Taoist teachings reflected a more conventional ethic. This is demonstrated in the *Hsiang-erh*, an early commentary on the *Tao Te Ching* that interprets the lack of benevolence of Heaven, Earth, and the sage to mean that Heaven, Earth, and the sage are benevolent to the good and not to the wicked. This and other texts affirmed the importance of following earlier ethics while at the same time incorporating new behavior. Adherents were to practice *wu-wei*; be weak (yielding) and supple; maintain their feminine nature; practice humility; and attain contentment and non-desire. Significantly, texts advocated filiality, loyalty, and benevolence—all Confucian virtues—and also prohibited curses, insults, breaking promises, theft, fornication, greed, hardheartedness, curiosity, gossip, and anger.

Ethical behavior was considered important for health and to ensure that rituals and practices of self-cultivation would be efficacious. Many ideas and aspects of the rituals from the early schools continue today. The Celestial Masters identified sin of both the individual and the individual's ancestors as the cause of illness and a shortened life-span. Rituals were believed to remove the stain of sin and encourage healing and longevity. Following rites of confession and repentance, misdeeds could be expiated by undertaking community service, such as repairing roads and providing food for the needy. Three times a year there were celebrations of the "Three Officials" (San Kuan), the deities of Heaven, Earth, and Water, who both recorded and forgave sins. Penitents confessed their sins on slips of paper which were then burned for the Official of Heaven, buried for the Official of Earth, and submerged for the Official of Water. Another rite, the Fast of Mud and Charcoal, extended its benefits universally: penitents asked for forgiveness for sins committed by themselves, their family members (both living and dead), all people, and all animals. Participants, having daubed their bodies with mud and charcoal, assumed the attitude of accused criminals during this ritual to expiate sins and promote healing.

The development of techniques of self-cultivation enhanced the importance of ethical principles. Ko Hung, whose fourth century work includes recipes for achieving immortality through the ingestion of alchemical elixirs (see pp.35–6), assumed that one must be morally and ritually pure for the substances and techniques to be effective. He held a common Taoist view that the "Three Worms," agents in the body that sap vitality, were spies that reported one's sins to Heaven, with every sin resulting in a predetermined reduction of life span. Wang Che, the founder of the Complete Perfection monastic order in the twelfth century (see p. 18), emphasized the importance of the ethics of the "Three Teachings"—Confucianism, Taoism, and Buddhism—in the pursuit of immortality through interior alchemy. He also prohibited sexual activity, alcohol, anger and desire for wealth.

敫火會雷運大然雷霆大作拆樹誅妖螺雨傾盆

*This illustration from a 19th-century Taoist weather manual depicts fire (*yang*) and cloud (*yin*) combined in a phase of evolving* ch'i, *or vital energy. Ink and cinnabar on paper.*

Admonitions for ethical behavior were also linked to recurrent millenarian expectations. Good works and confession for the forgiveness of sins were believed to hasten the coming of a perfect world. Believers anticipated that a cataclysm would result from accumulated evil, and that this would be followed by the appearance of a savior, often identified as Lord Lao. After the destruction of all non-believers, there would be an era of peace, prosperity, and longevity. Good works and ethical behavior were thus linked to bringing about a perfected world as well as perfected individuals.

The basic themes of early Taoist ethics are still expressed today. The practices of self-cultivation are continued by priests, who bring renewal and healing to communities as well as to individuals. The benefit conferred on the community by priestly ritual is most eloquently expressed in the great *chiao* ceremony. Dating from the fifth century CE, the *chiao* is known for its beautiful vestments, elaborate altarpieces, and powerful music. It is usually performed around the time of the winter solstice, when the creative *yang* force is believed to be on the verge of renewal. Priests involved in the *chiao* must be ritually pure to ensure that the cosmic powers, envisioned as the Three Pure Ones (see p.27), will descend.

In the sacred space created for the *chiao*, the priest first paces out the world in miniature. During the ceremony itself, the energies of the cosmos are realized in the high priest's body. The Taoist theme of returning to the origin in order to achieve renewal is central to the ceremony: the priest aims to bring about the replenishment of the forces of light, life, blessing, growth, and *yang* for the entire community, both living and dead.

Precepts for Becoming an Immortal

❝ Do not permit your heart to contain wicked and jealous feelings. Do not allow crafty and treacherous thoughts to grow and come forth from you. ...

Preserve your humaneness, and do not kill. ... Have compassion and love for all. ...

Preserve your purity, and expound on righteousness. Do not engage in debauchery, do not live in excess. ...

Limit alcohol. Regulate your behavior. Be harmonious in energy and disposition. Do not damage your inner spirit. Do not commit any of the multitude of evils.

Do not criticize or argue about the scriptures and teachings. Do not detest the sages' writings. ... Always act as though you were face to face with the gods.

Be wholehearted and uniform in your deportment and all your actions. Be certain that all your actions between both humans and gods are harmonious and conciliatory. ❞

From *T'ai-shang tung-hsüan ling-pao ch'ih-shu yü-chüeh miao-ching* [*Red Writings and Jade Mysteries*], translated by Jennifer Oldstone-Moore.

Commentary

In the schools of religious Taoism, secret teachings and practices could only be revealed to those who were deemed worthy. A kind of predestination was assumed: the only persons who were permitted to follow the advanced path of the adept were those whose names were written in the celestial registers and who already had "jade bones"—bones made from the incorruptible material that provided a framework for the immortal body that was to be cultivated. However, even with this inheritance, an adept had to live a pure and moral life and to follow esoteric practices in order to become an Immortal. Moral codes often include lists of precepts, vows, and rules. Ethical behavior was an integral part of the overall discipline to which adepts adhered in order to purify their hearts, minds, and bodies.

This excerpt is from one of the texts of the Numinous Jewel school, dating from the late fourth or early fifth century CE. The precepts also act as vows which are taken by adepts who are setting out on their journey to lead the life of the Taoist. The text shows influence from the "Five Precepts" of Buddhism (which prohibit killing, stealing, lying, improper sexual behavior, and intoxicating beverages) and from the Buddhist call to universal salvation and compassion.

CHAPTER SIX

SACRED SPACE

In the Chinese worldview, the cosmos is a sacred place, fundamentally interrelated, holy, and complete. Self-creating and self-sustaining, the cosmos evolves and decays in a ceaseless pattern, and all individual manifestations within it are structured according to this pattern. For this reason, the body is perceived as a sacred microcosm—those who follow the Tao can align themselves with the flow of cosmic power and strive to cultivate and purify the universe within their bodies.

Of particular significance to Taoism are geographical features such as rivers, mountains, and caves. Temples and shrines are often erected on or near these sacred spaces. Taoists consider it beneficial to make pilgrimages to such sites, either in person, or through visualization, in the microcosm of one's body.

LEFT: The spectacular, pine-clad mountainscape of southern Anhui province. In Taoism, mountains are traditionally revered as places of special power, where ch'i, *or "vital energy," is particularly strong.*

In Taoism, the universe is connected and unitary, for all creation emanates from and is shaped by the Tao, which is before time or creation. From the chaotic but fertile Tao comes *ch'i*, or "vital matter," in its primordial state. It is divided into *yin ch'i*, which is heavy and sinks down, and *yang ch'i*, which is light and ascends. From this basic binary relationship the universe is created, manifest in a variety of groupings and divisions. Of these, pentads, or groupings of five, came to be particularly significant, with the "Five Phases" (*wu-hsing*) becoming a powerful organizing principle for Chinese and Taoist thinking. The Five Phases (also known as the "Five Elements" or "Agents") articulate *ch'i* as greater and lesser *yin* (water and metal), greater and lesser *yang* (fire and wood), and a balanced center (earth). These phases are related through patterns that are mutually engendering (wood-fire-earth-metal-water) and mutually destructive (fire-water-earth-wood-metal). Their basic qualities and modes of interaction are used as a highly abstract framework to understand and explain the workings of virtually everything, from the rise and fall of dynasties and the workings of internal organs to the passage of time.

All things, from spirits to rocks, are made of the same material, *ch'i*. There are some places where *ch'i* can be found in great quantity and with exceptional quality; it flows through channels and grids in the earth, giving life and energy to all creatures. Mountains are among such places, and have been venerated from ancient times in China, both as deities and as meeting places between the human and the divine. Central to Taoism, they are the source of herbs and minerals for elixirs and medicines, and are reputed to be the homes of Immortals. Both the human body and the ritual altar are conceptualized as mountains in Taoist ritual practices.

The "Five Sacred Peaks" resonate with the symbolism of the Five Phases. These mountains—T'ai, Heng, Heng (a different place), Hua, and Sung—are important to Chinese religions in general, and have been favored retreats of Taoists and the sites of numerous temples and monasteries. Other important mountains include those identified with specific schools, such as Mount Mao (Shang-ch'ing), Mount Lung-hu (Celestial Masters), and Mount Wu-tang (home to the Taoist martial arts' school). Some sacred mountains—for example, Mount K'un-lun, the home of the Queen Mother of the West—are mythical (there is a range by that name, but it is not the same place).

Mountains form a network of sacred sites with grottoes and blessed realms. Grottoes, literally "cave heavens," were thought to be illuminated by their own light or by light from heaven. They were also considered sources

A *Taoist shrine in the Huang Shan, the range where the Yellow Emperor is said to have ascended to immortality.*

of vitalizing energy, places of the gods, and were even seen as sacred microcosms, worlds within themselves. Blessed realms also dotted the landscape. Taoists designated and mapped ten great grotto heavens, thirty-six smaller grotto heavens, and seventy-two blessed realms. These were understood to be connected by subterranean passageways, forming a grid of sacred places and power.

These ideas are related to the ancient art of *feng-shui*, another means of accessing cosmic power. While not strictly Taoist, *feng-shui* (literally, "wind and water") is the art of fixing the most auspicious place for graves, buildings, and even cities, in order to make the most of the *ch'i* present in the environment and to live harmoniously within the natural order. The *feng-shui* master uses a special compass to take bearings on the site and on visible features of the surrounding landscape—such as mountain peaks, watercourses, paths, and prominent rocks—to determine the auspiciousness of the site.

Channels of energy can be accessed and put to use through *feng-shui*; similarly, the channels of *ch'i* in the body can be manipulated to advantage through practices such as acupuncture. The parallel between the inner and outer worlds is drawn in elaborate detail. Certain Taoist meditative practices instruct the adept to look inward and observe the "country of the body." This "country" is a sacred microcosm, a faithful duplication of the universe: it has the same structure and features as the cosmos, and is replete with gods, mountains, constellations and heavenly bodies, bridges, lakes and pagodas, and perhaps the "embryo of immortality". It is inhabited by a large population which is administered in the same way as the imperial Chinese state. The prince of the body is found in the heart; his ministers and subordinates manage and govern throughout the body. State, cosmos, and body are all understood to be structured in homologous ways, creating concentric units of sacred space. These units interpenetrate each other— as, for example, in the actions and liturgy of the *chiao* ceremony (see p.59), where the priest simultaneously renews the community and cultivates his "immortal embryo."

The true form of the macrocosm is also presented in the microcosm of sacred drawings, such as talismans and diagrams. These show the internal structure of powerful sources of cosmic energy. By knowing their true form, adepts have control over these sources of power. Diagrams show the true shape of mountains, grottoes, and other geographical features, thus protecting the adept from any dangers that might exist there, such as demons or evil spirits. Talismans, which resemble complex Chinese characters in an archaic style, can portray the sacred places of the body and the cosmos, providing important knowledge to those who would traverse them. Talismans are usually linked to oral formulas that are only given to the initiated to make them efficacious.

Taoist sacred space includes temples and monasteries. Most temples in China are neighborhood temples run by lay people, and are not specifically Taoist. They house images of Taoist deities, such as the Three Pure Ones, as well as other popular spirits, including the Eight Immortals, Kuan-ti, tutelary gods, and figures from the Confucian and Buddhist traditions. Taoist priests may be hired at such temples for ritual purposes. There are also specifically Taoist structures, such as the White Cloud Abbey in Peking (Beijing), a monastery of the Complete Truth school. Eastern Peak (Tung-yüeh) temples, associated with the Orthodox Unity school, have separate chambers that depict the torments and tormenters of Hell as found under Mount T'ai, the eastern peak. Lay people present sacrifices at specific chambers in these temples in order to speed the soul of loved ones through judgment and punishment.

Other temples are often situated near natural features, such as holy mountains, that have spiritual significance—many of these have become notable pilgrimage centers. Some temples and abbeys received imperial patronage. During the T'ang dynasty (618–907CE), shrines and monasteries were established on numerous sacred peaks and at sites where famous Taoists had "obtained the Way." One monastery, Tower Abbey, was founded on the site where Lao-tzu is said to have revealed the *Tao Te Ching*—it became a dynastic cult center, and was renamed the Abbey of the Holy Ancestor.

Women Pilgrims to Mount T'ai

❝ The laywoman said: 'My dear—could there be another T'ai Shan in the world? From the top you get a perfect view of all the lands on earth, the dragons' palaces, ocean treasures, Buddhas' halls, and immortals' palaces. If such benefits were not to be had, why would men and women come thousands of miles from their homes? ... What's more, Our Lady of T'ai Shan controls life and death, luck and prosperity for people through all the world. ... The reverent at heart, when they come before Our Lady, see the goddess's true face in the flesh; if not reverent at heart, the face they see is only a gilded face. She is powerful and effective for bringing good luck and forgiving misdeeds. And on the mountain there is no end of wonderful sights, like the South-facing Cave, the Three Heavenly Gates, the Yellow Flower Island, the Platform of Suicides, the Rock for Drying Scriptures, the Stele without Inscription, the Pine of Ch'in, the Cypress of Han, the Golden Slips, the Jade Writings—all these are where the gods and immortals make their dwelling. No one with only average luck could ever get to go there!' **❞**

From *Hsing-shih yin-yuan chuan* by Hsi Chou Sheng, translated by Glen Dudbridge in Susan Naquin and Chün-fang Yü, eds., *Pilgrims and Sacred Sites in China*, University of California Press, 1992, p.46.

Commentary

Taoist adepts were avid pilgrims, but they were by no means the only ones who were interested in embarking on sacred journeys. People from all levels of society went on pilgrimages. Emperors demonstrated their sovereignty through their journeys to sacred spots; common people asked for blessings and forgiveness when they reached their destination, or else they traveled to these places in order to see famous sights, as this passage indicates. Of all the sacred peaks, Mount T'ai (T'ai Shan) has loomed the largest in Chinese religious history. The god of Mount T'ai became an important figure in the celestial bureaucracy, subordinate only to the Jade Emperor. He was in charge of regulating birth, death, and human achievements.

In this story, from the seventeenth or eighteenth century, pilgrims are there not only to sight-see but to ask favors of Our Lady of T'ai Shan, the daughter of the god of Mount T'ai. Known to the Chinese as Pi-hsia yüan-chün, the Sovereign of the Clouds at Dawn, she became the most popular female Taoist deity in late imperial China. In her compassion and concern for humble people, she resembles Kuan-yin, the Buddhist goddess of mercy. Mount T'ai, its hundreds of shrines and its ascent of 7,000 rock-cut steps remain much visited to this day.

CHAPTER SEVEN

SACRED TIME

Taoists are masters of time as well as space. Their activities reveal their desire to align with the rhythms of the cosmos and with cycles of time that are discernible in the abstract patterns of *yin* and *yang* and the "Five Phases," which explain the workings of time as well as matter. Taoist ritual is based on detailed knowledge of these rhythms, and is formulated either to accelerate time, to bring precious materials (eg., metals) to fruition, or to trace it backward, to return to the moment of creation and to the life-giving original *ch'i* that will confer immortality.

The patterns of *yin* and *yang* and the Five Phases are also central to pan-Chinese religious festivals. Although not exclusively Taoist, these festivals reflect Taoist beliefs and serve as popular expressions of the tradition's approach to the concepts of time, nature, and destiny.

*LEFT:
A Taoist priest officiates at the Hungry Ghosts' festival in Penang, Malaysia. The statues represent ghosts, and it is believed that they come to Earth for one month every year to enjoy good food and entertainment.*

In Taoist reckoning, the primordial Tao existed before time, which was not set into motion until after the emergence of primordial *ch'i*. The pattern of time is thus a part of the unfolding of creation—it is to be identified, learned, and used to one's benefit. This is the basis of most Taoist practice, and is made explicit in "external" and "internal alchemy." In external alchemy (now defunct), adepts controlled time to accelerate the purification of materials that confer immortality. In internal alchemy, the flow of vital essences in the body are reversed in order to reverse the passage and effects of time and return to the state of the newborn, who is full of vital energies. This primal vitality is manifest in the "embryo of immortality" created by such practices. The alchemist, echoing and manipulating the cosmic flow, produces microcosms in time as well as in space. (See also pp.90–91.)

Other practices also correspond to the cosmic movement of time: adepts in Taoist monasteries rise and retire with the sun; and the *chiao* festival of renewal (see p.59) is usually performed around the winter solstice to coincide with the rebirth of *yang* that occurs during this period. The celebrations and observances surrounding the Chinese religious year reflect a similar recognition of the variable characteristics of time—this is evident in the attention that is paid to the cycles of *yin* and *yang* and the "Five Phases" (see p.64). Although not strictly Taoist, they reflect Taoist sensibilities, and Taoist priests may officiate at rituals associated with festivals.

Chinese time is observed according to both the lunar and solar calendars. The lunar calendar is twelve months, with a thirteenth month added every two or three years. In the solar calendar, "nodes," or "breaths," refer to the twenty-four periods of approximately fifteen days into which the year is divided. These divisions correspond to the patterns of the agricultural year. The start of each season in the solar year is determined by the solstices and equinoxes.

Years are then organized into cycles. First, there is the cycle of twelve years, familiar to many from the animals of the Chinese zodiac. This scheme of twelve is then widened into a sixty-year cycle, characterized by two sets of symbols—the "Ten Heavenly Stems" and the "Twelve Earthly Branches." Each animal in the zodiac is associated with one branch. The cycle is completed by associating each stem with one of the "Five Colors" (which correspond to the Five Phases), with two stems per color. The end result is a cycle of sixty, and each animal will be linked with each color once in the cycle. *Chia-tzu*, the year of the Blue Rat, is the first year of the sixty-year cycle.

Many festivals in the Chinese religious year coincide with significant phases of the moon; others are derived from the agricultural cycle. Annual festivals reflect ancient *yin-yang* and Five-Phase cosmology, corresponding to the phases of the moon, the change of seasons, and movements in the heavens. Holidays frequenly fall on days with *yang* symbolism (odd numbers are *yang*) or on the full moon (the fifteenth of each lunar month). These festivals demonstrate a number of significant themes: the importance of the family and the respect shown for forebears; the pursuit of longevity; the desire for blessings; and the propitiation and warding-off of potentially malevolent forces. The festal year includes the worship of the gods and goddesses of the popular religion, particularly in the celebrations to mark their birthdays.

The New Year, or Spring Festival, is the most important holiday in the Chinese calendar. It is a time of beginnings and family reunions. Families sweep out the old with housecleaning, the settling of debts, and the completion of unsettled business. This period is a celebration of the return of *yang* after the winter solstice—*yang* colors (red, gold, and orange) are seen everywhere, particularly in paper decorations and in round foods such as oranges and kumquats (round signifies comple-

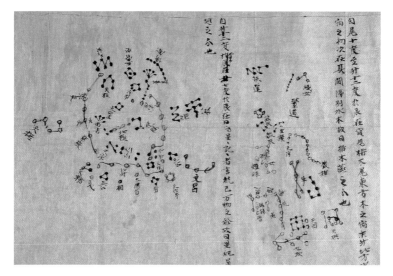

A star map of ca.940CE. For millennia, Chinese astronomer-scribes produced such maps, providing China with the world's most complete records of unusual celestial phenomena.

tion). Ideally, the family comes together on New Year's Eve, and all are careful not to mar the family's fortune for the coming year with cross words or with actions that may be deemed to be unlucky.

New Year festivities end on the fifteenth day of the first month with the Lantern Festival. During the two weeks of celebrations, many popular gods receive offerings. The last day of the holiday is also the birthday of the "Official of Heaven," one of the "Three Officials" (see p.56)—sacrifices to him are presented at dawn on this day. Another major festival is Ch'ing-ming ("Clear and Bright") which is a time to revive ties with the dead and to celebrate renewal of the family, symbolized by the new life of spring (the festival falls two weeks after the spring equinox).

The Double Fifth festival observes the peak of *yang* at the summer solstice on the fifth day of the fifth lunar month. Any excess, whether of *yin* or *yang*, is considered dangerous (an excess of *yang* is evident in heat and epidemics). Protection is therefore sought at this time by the display of pungent herbs or plants with shapes that resemble sharp weapons. The "Five Poisons" (centipede, snake, scorpion, toad, and lizard) and the "Five Colors" (blue, red, yellow, white, and black) are also believed to offer protection—the former are thought to fend off danger with their toxins and are represented on clothing, food, and amulets; the latter are said to summon forth the power of the "Five Phases."

The Double Fifth also celebrates dragons, water, and a famous poet. During this season, rice seedlings are transplanted into paddies and watered by heavy rains. According to Chinese tradition, this rain is caused by dragons who live in the clouds and who water and bless the Earth with fertility. The "dragon boat" races that are held on the Double Fifth reflect not only this lore but also the legend of Ch'ü Yüan, a poet who served in the government during the Chou dynasty. When his advice was disregarded, he threw himself into a river in despair. Today's dragon boat races reenact the frantic search for him that took place.

The Feast of the Hungry Ghosts on the fifteenth day of the seventh lunar month focuses on communal protection, which is provided, in part, by the ritual actions of Taoist priests. During this month, the gates of Hell are opened, and its residents are free to wander at will. Those with no descendants to care for them (euphemistically called "the good brethren") are malevolent, unhappy, and potentially dangerous ghosts. The festival is designed to placate such beings with things they may need, such as sustenance and amusements, including music and theater. On Hungry Ghosts' day, a community celebration at an outdoor altar is conducted by both Taoist and Buddhist priests who exhort the ghosts to repent and end their sufferings in the underworld. Ghosts who do not repent are sent back to Hell after the ceremony.

The Chinese celebration of the harvest, the Mid-Autumn festival, falls at full moon in the eighth lunar month, when *yang* has completed its dominance and gives way to *yin* after the autumnal equinox. Chinese tell the story of the rabbit in the moon, who is pounding the ingredients for the elixir of immortality with a pestle, and of Ch'ang-o, the woman who drank the elixir intended for her husband and floated up to the moon where she has lived ever since. A festival less frequently observed today is the Double Nine. This number evokes the symbolism of *yang*: nine is the most *yang* of numbers and double *yang* is seen as especially auspicious. It is also the time, just after the autumnal equinox, when *yin* has begun to prevail. Traditionally, the day has been celebrated by drinking chrysanthemum wine and taking mountain hikes, the late autumn blossom symbolizing long life.

The timing of family rites is structurally similar to the timing of festivals and reflects the fluctuation of *yin* and *yang* and the cycles of the Five Phases. In this way, Taoist thinking and practice pervades Chinese life. Taoists may be called upon to determine auspicious days for important events, and to assist in rituals, as need arises. Weddings are a primary means of ensuring the continuation of the family line, a major consideration in Chinese culture. Families must match the bride's and groom's horoscopes to determine their relationship to each other vis-à-vis cosmic time. Before a couple is betrothed, an astrologer will check the "eight characters," the year, month, day, and hour of birth of both parties in order to confirm their compatibility. The almanac remains an important source for selecting the appropriate day. The positioning of the bride's and the groom's families at the various ceremonies of betrothal and marriage reflect *yin* and *yang* relationships, with the bride's family on the west side, and the groom's on the east.

A new mother, having observed various folk traditions during pregnancy to protect the fetus and ensure an easy birth, will "sit the month" after childbirth. This means that she stays at home, where she is nourished by "warm" or *yang* foods and by a soup that provides five medicinal herbs, one for each of the Five Phases.

The rites of passage associated with death use the symbolic language of *yin* and *yang* in the ritual placement of mourners at the funeral: women are placed to the west and men to the east. The same symbolism is also evident in the preparation of the corpse for burial—for example, soon after death, the corpse is oriented with its head toward the south to denote fire (and therefore purification); similarly, the family's grief is expressed by draping the family alter with white (*yin*) coverings—this denotes death, the west, and final rest. Periods of crisis and celebration in the family are thus integrated into larger cycles of time and change, easing transition and ensuring the efficacy of rituals.

The Management of Time

❝ Natural cyclically transformed elixir is formed when flowing mercury, embracing Squire Metal [i.e. lead], becomes pregnant. Wherever there is cinnabar there are also lead and silver. In 4,320 years the elixir is finished ... It embraces the *ch'i* of sun and moon, *yin* and *yang*, for 4,320 years; thus, upon repletion of its own *ch'i*, it becomes a cyclically transformed elixir for immortals of the highest grade and for celestial beings. When in the world below lead and mercury are subjected to the alchemical process for purposes of immortality, [the elixir] is finished in one year. ... ❞

From the *Heart-Mirror of Mnemonics and Explanations from Writings on the Elixir* translated by Nathan Sivin in N. Sivin, "Chinese Alchemy and the Manipulation of Time" in N Sivin, ed., *Science and Technology in East Asia.* New York: Science History Publications, 1977, p.112.

❝ As for the time of firing the furnace, the fire should be applied at a midnight which is also the first hour of a sixty-hour cycle, on the first day of a sixty-day cycle, in the eleventh month [i.e. the month which contains the winter solstice]. Begin by firing through door A for 5 days, using 3oz of charcoal... Then open door B and start the fire, firing for 5 days, using 4 oz of charcoal. Then open door C and start the fire, firing for 5 days, using 5oz of charcoal. ❞

From *Arcane Teachings on the Ninefold Cyclically Transfromed Gold Elixir* translated by Nathan Sivin in N. Sivin, "Chinese Alchemy and the Manipulation of Time" in N Sivin, ed., *Science and Technology in East Asia.* New York: Science History Publications, 1977, p.115.

Commentary

Control of time is essential in transmuting materials into the "elixir of immortality" (see p.36). The genius of the Taoist alchemist lies in the mastery of the inter-related material, spatial, and temporal aspects of the Tao in the cosmos and the ability to recreate these patterns to nurture one's own body. To hasten the manufacture of potable gold that could be made into an elixir of immortality, alchemists recreated the cosmos in minia-ture in the laboratory, exhibiting their knowledge of the pattern of change through time that occurs in the unfolding of the Tao. (See also pp.90–91.)

In the first extract (opposite, written before 900CE), the alchemist's knowledge of the Tao is used to telescope time in the laboratory. Each day is divided into twelve "hours"—a lunar year of 360 days has 4,320 such hours. One hour in the laboratory was deemed to have the same effect on the metal as one year in the earth.

The second extract, from a manual by the alchemist Chen Shao-wei, ca. 712CE, reveals the care that is taken to mimic the fluctuation of *yin* and *yang* in a calendar year. "Fire phasing" correlated with cosmic cycles, and recre-ated, in miniature, the ebb and flow of heat across the seasons of a year. Thus discernment of temporal patterns was necessary to gaining spiritual and physical benefits.

CHAPTER EIGHT

DEATH AND THE AFTERLIFE

Taoist responses to death vary, but all address the concept of change. Priests help effect the transformation of a dead family member into a benevolent ancestor. Without such a change he or she could become a dangerous ghost.

Some people strive to escape death altogether. Chinese notions of immortality assume the need for a physical body; Taoist practices are therefore directed at refining one's body so as to return it to a condition of undifferentiated potential—like the Tao before creation. In these practices, adepts use cosmic powers and mastery of time and matter to attain deathlessness. Immortals revel in their release from the constraints of human existence. In contrast, a few Taoists marvel at the pattern of creation and destruction, relishing freedom from the fear of death and change more than freedom from death itself.

LEFT: A Ch'ing dynasty illustration depicting a figure, probably an Immortal, ascending to a celestial palace. From Keepsake from the Cloud Gallery, *or* Yün t'ai hsien jui *(1750), a text describing the practices of a Tao adept.*

Chinese ideas about the soul and its fate date from ancient times, but were never organized into a single, definitive system. Sources describe two kinds of soul, usually designated as the *hun* and the *p'o*. The actual number of *hun* and *p'o* souls residing in a person is disputed. Souls are made of the same vital material, *ch'i*, as all other things, and thus the boundaries between the living and the dead are relatively fluid. The *hun* soul is made of *yang ch'i* and represents the spiritual and intellectual aspects; the *p'o* consists of *yin ch'i*, which is the bodily, animating principle. At death, the *hun* soul departs from the body and ascends, the *p'o* soul sinks into the ground. Funerary rituals are performed to settle the *hun* soul into the ancestral tablets that are found on the domestic altar of many Chinese homes; they also ensure that the *p'o* soul will settle peacefully into the grave.

Beliefs about death and the afterlife draw from the various traditions of Chinese religion, and thus can encompass numerous—and, in some cases, apparently contradictory—notions of one's fate after death. In addition to being settled in the gravesite and in the ancestor tablets, the soul of the deceased is believed to descend into the Chinese underworld, or Hell, to be tried by the infernal judiciary. Important Buddhist concepts were integrated with indigenous Chinese ideas, including the idea of *karma* (an individual's balance of accumulated merits and demerits); the figure of Yama, the king of Hell; and the different punishment levels of Hell, in which sinners suffer to redress their karmic imbalance before being reincarnated on earth.

Like its celestial counterpart, Hell is structured in the same way as the old Chinese imperial bureaucracy and judiciary. On entering it, souls are judged by the Ten Magistrates who preside over the Ten Tribunals of Hell. The books of life and death, in which every person's alloted days are recorded, are managed by this bureaucracy, and Chinese folklore contains many accounts of bureaucractic mistakes that result in a person being wrongly brought to death and judgment until the error is discovered. After judgment, the soul pays for its past crimes by passing through various layers of Hell, where it undergoes torments appropriate to the crimes committed. At last, the soul reaches the final court where, having atoned for shortcomings in the life just past, it is reincarnated in accordance with the merits it has accumulated in its previous existence.

Taoist priests play an important role in death ritual. As officials of the spirit world, Taoists are able to prepare and present the proper documents to the appropriate bureaucrats in the underworld. They are hired by the bereaved to ensure that the soul of a beloved family member spends a minimal amount of time suffering for any misdeeds. The funeral ritual may include the sending of a special document, a writ of pardon, and the drama of the deliverance of the soul from punishment in Hell.

Taoist priests are also important in communicating with the dead and restoring harmony in the family. After the body has been appropriately buried, it is the responsibility of the living to provide the things the dead will need to be comfortable: food, money, and other amenities. For family members, this means daily offerings of incense and periodic offerings of food, drink, and spirit money. Should there be discord or ill fortune in the family, a Taoist priest may be summoned to determine if the family is suffering on account of a discontented ancestor. He—for the individual is invariably male—may then diagnose the appropriate actions to be taken to pacify the unhappy spirit and restore harmony to the family.

Throughout its long history, Taoism has also developed elaborate techniques to escape death altogether. Methods for achieving immortality include both tempering the physical body and purifying one's heart and mind, as there was no radical dichotomy between body and soul. Belief in the possibility of immortality is not exclusively Taoist—however, the schools of Taoism have system-

A sculpture representing a spirit at East Mountain Temple, Tainan, Taiwan. Identified with Mount T'ai, the temple recreates in its statuary the places of judgment and punishment.

atized various techniques. These include meditation, visualization and breathing exercises, gymnastics, sexual practices, dietary control, and concocting special medicines. In ancient times, people sought the elixir or pill of immortality, either in their own laboratories, or from individuals who lived in legendary places at the edges of the known world, such as the Queen Mother of the West (see p.28 and pp.30–31).

A famous Taoist concerned with these practices was Ko Hung (see p.35), whose text *Pao-p'u tzu* has a number of recipes for pills that confer immortality. Especially prized ingredients by alchemists included gold, which does not corrode and is thus associated with immutability, arsenic and lead, and cinnabar, a form of mercury, valued for its red (*yang*) color and because it easily transmutes into various forms (see pp.82–3). Such medicines were very costly. This "external alchemy" correlated the transformations of chemical substances in the laboratory to transformations in the cosmos and the body. The knowledge needed to unlock the secrets of how to change chemical matter was the same knowledge needed to halt the decay and deterioration brought about by old age. Many emperors were eager adepts of external alchemy, and it is thought that, ironically, several may have been poisoned by the medicines.

By the eighth or ninth century, the practice of external alchemy had been interiorized, so that the language of refining and transmuting gold and cinnabar was now used to denote elements and transformations in the crucible of the body (rather than the laboratory). Practitioners of internal alchemy sought the coalescence of purified and perfected bodily essences—such as sexual fluids, saliva, and *ch'i*—into an "embryo of immortality." Also called the "Red Child," this "holy embryo" was established in the belly of the adept, where, properly nourished through correct practices, it would develop into a perfected body, an immortal, true, real self that would replace the adept's old, corruptible body. Internal alchemy continues to be a defining aspect of Taoist practice to this day.

The assumption underlying all such practices is the correlation of the microcosmic body to the macrocosmic universe. The adept must identify and preserve the "primordial breath" (*yüan ch'i*) that corresponds to the life-giving, undifferentiated Tao at the beginning of creation. The adept works to retain the vital bodily essences of breath, life force, and spirit, and end the gradual depletion of these essences that leads ultimately to death. Many practices involve reversing, through visualization, the usual flow of bodily fluids, such as sexual fluids, and, in so doing, reverse the effects of time.

In meditation and visualization exercises, the practitioner focuses on the Tao and on powerful gods that reside in Heaven and the body. Breathing techniques aim to produce "embryonic" breathing—breathing that is so slow and shallow that a feather placed on an adept's nose will remain motionless. Purification of the breath and body are enhanced by a special diet, which may include the consumption of foods associated with long life, including certain mushrooms, pine seeds, and pine sap; and the avoidance of foods, especially cereals, that nourish the malevolent and destructive spirits in the body such as the "Three Worms" (see p.57). Sexual techniques aim to control orgasm, which is believed to cause devastating depletion of vital essences, and enable one to benefit from the *yin* or *yang* essence of one's partner. Gymnastic exercises, such as *ch'i-kung* and *t'ai-ch'i ch'üan*, both conserve essences and ensure the proper circulation for maximum strength and benefit.

These practices are largely physiological procedure and effect—it is, however, taken for granted that they will be supplemented by a moral lifestyle. Evil and immoral deeds shorten the lifespan as a consequence of reports to celestial gods such as the Three Officials; they may also cause the gods who reside in one's body to depart, hastening or even causing death. In addition to leading a moral life, adepts require a skilled master who can train them in the secret texts and oral instructions that complement the esoteric and opaque written formulae. Those who have the will and ability to complete these rigorous courses join the ranks of the Immortals, living in mountains and grottoes, flying among the stars, and wandering the earth in perfect serenity, nourished by eating the wind and drinking the dew.

Few have the stamina to become Immortals, fewer still embrace death without fear. A distinctive attitude toward death and the afterlife is notable in the earliest texts of Taoism, especially in the compelling stories of Chuang-tzu (see pp.34–5). He speculates on the possibility that we may find death preferable to life and claims that our fate is no more than to continue in the process of coagulation and the dissipation of *ch'i* amid the eternal flux that brought us into being; we can never leave the bosom of the Tao. From this perspective, death and life are but alternating parts of a cycle—they are to be neither sought nor feared. Some of Chuang-tzu's most moving and memorable passages celebrate death in this way: marveling at the unique, creative possibilities of transformation during death and life, while "dwelling in the greatest of mansions," the universe which follows the pattern of the Tao.

Secrets of Immortality from *Journey to the West*

❝ You must completely grasp this important secret ...
Spare and cultivate the life forces ...
All is composed of semen, breath and spirit,
Be cautious; make them secure; stop all leakage.

Stop all leakage, preserve them in the body,
Accept my teachings and the Way will flourish. ...
They remove evil desires, lead to purity.

They lead to purity, bright and lustrous,
You can face the Cinnabar Platform and enjoy
the bright moon.
The moon holds the Jade Rabbit; the sun
holds the Raven,
From there also the Tortoise and Snake,
coiled together.

Coiled together, the life forces are strong,
You can plant the golden lotus in the midst of the fire.
Assemble the Five Phases; reverse them to use them,
This work complete, you can be a buddha or an
immortal as you wish. **❞**

From *Hsi-yu chi* [*Jouney to the West*] by Wu Ch'eng-en. Taipei: Sheng-yang ch'u-pan she, 1988, p.13.
Translated by Jennifer Oldstone-Moore.

Commentary

This passage is from *Journey to the West*, also known as *Monkey*, a highly entertaining novel written in 1592 by Wu Ch'eng-en. Still read in China today, it tells the story of a Buddhist monk and his four disciples on a pilgrimage to India. But this popular tale can also be read as an allegory of Taoist immortality, Buddhist enlightenment and Confucian mind-cultivation (all of which have been attained by the end of the novel). Much of the text is loaded with symbolism, taking place in the body of an adept and containing subtle references to Taoist practices throughout. The story shows the way in which the "Three Teachings" of Taoism, Buddhism, and Confucianism are embraced simultaneously.

This poem from the novel relates to the Taoist initiation of Monkey (one of the book's principal characters and the best of the disciples), who has been deemed worthy to receive the secret teachings from a Taoist patriarch. The verse contains many alchemical references: conserving and purifying bodily fluids; symbols such as the snake and tortoise used by Taoists to denote *yin* and *yang*; and the reversal of the "Five Phases" (see pp.64–5) to reverse the effects of time, an indication of the Way which leads ultimately to the transcending of death and the attainment of immortality.

CHAPTER NINE

SOCIETY AND RELIGION

The effect of Taoism on Chinese culture has been profound. Its wide-ranging influence has extended to philosophy, medicine, and government, and has provided an emphasis on the feminine in an otherwise male-oriented culture. The fine arts also often reflect the Taoist ideals of spontaneity, appreciation of nature, and retreat from the world.

Taoist practices have been integrated into society at the very highest levels, influencing emperors, controlling contact with the spirit world, and providing important rituals. Taoism's massive collection of scriptures and its highly trained priesthood distinguish it from the popular tradition, but the close connections that exist between the two are manifested regularly at the community temples, where the effect Taoism has had on ordinary people is revealed.

LEFT:
A worshiper with incense sticks. Incense, more than simply a fragrant offering, is a symbol of the Three Primary Vitalities ("original" breath, essence and spirit), and is believed to draw deities to the altar.

Despite its inherent mysticism, the *Tao Te Ching* is a treatise on government. The ideal ruler portrayed within its pages is so subtle and inconspicuous that his subjects are unaware of being ruled; his statesmanship eradicates distinctions that cause envy and discontent so that people have no superfluous desires. Although this ideal Taoist state has never been put into practice, the role of Taoism in government has nevertheless been manifest in a variety of ways.

At the end of the second century CE, Taoism was implemented as a theocracy mandated by Lord Lao (the divinized Lao-tzu). Confession and absolution by Taoist gods was established by the Celestial Masters in the third century (see pp.16–17). The new state, founded in modern-day Szechwan, was divided into 24 districts which were overseen by a Taoist official and protected by the gods and spiritual beings under his or her command. The Celestial Master government did not last as an autonomous force. However, in ceding civil authority to a political leader, it established a precedent whereby leading Taoist figures became sources of legitimization for kings and emperors who were then sanctioned by Lord Lao. This relationship was especially cultivated in the Period of Disunity, and in the T'ang and Sung dynasties. State patronage often included the establishment of new temples which not only enhanced Taoism but also bolstered imperial prestige.

From the beginning of organized Taoism, the tradition provided elements of messianic and millenarian expectation—this threatened the status quo and raised government suspicions. Taoist imagery and ideas were used in various rebellions. Among these was a series of revolts connected with the figure Li Hung, who instigated an uprising in the fourth century which was based on a prophecy that he would become king—because of his family name, Li, he was believed to be a manifestation of Lao-tzu, and it was anticipated that he would bring about a utopian age.

Taoism's relationship with the present government of the People's Republic of China is uncertain: only the monastic Taoism of the Complete Perfection school is officially recognized. Other Taoist practices are categorized as "superstitions" and are actively discouraged.

The tradition has also long been associated with the healing arts. The goals and methods of traditional Chinese medicine and Taoism overlap: Chinese medicine is centered on the healthy circulation of *ch'i*, the balance of *yin* and *yang* in the body, and the use of various substances to nourish the body. These theories also inform the Taoist quest for immortality. Taoist alchemy has been

Taoist orthodox priests take part in a festival in Taiwan. Vestments and texts are passed down from father to son.

described as a protoscience, and attempts by Taoist alchemists to produce the "elixir of immortality" (see p.90) led to other significant discoveries—notably, the invention of gunpowder.

Other Taoist forms of healing reflected the role of the Taoist priest as an authority over spirits. These included faith-healing through the confession of sins and forgiveness from the celestial administrators of life and death; exorcism; and the preparation of talismans for therapeutic medicine. The tradition also developed therapeutic and longevity exercises such as *ch'i-kung* and *t'ai-chi ch'üan*.

Such practices are related to the martial arts, which work to cultivate bodily strength through moral behavior, focused attention, and the conservation and strengthening of *ch'i*. Two notable Taoist martial arts' schools are the Shao-lin and Wu-tang.

Taoism has had a tremendous effect on the fine arts, including poetry, theatre, painting, and calligraphy. The naturalistic mysticism of Lao-tzu, Chuang-tzu, and Huai-nan-tzu is evident in Chinese painting. Many famous landscape painters of the Sung and Yüan dynasties, such as Fan K'uan, were Taoist-style recluses and eccentrics. His famous landscapes portray Taoist ideas of the relative importance of humans to nature: humans are depicted as minute beings in contrast to the vastness of nature. Calligraphy, the most cherished visual art in China, is closely linked to Taoist ideals of spontenaeity while following the natural pattern: calligraphers must be both perfectly controlled and perfectly spontaneous while exercising their art. Taoist talismans are a special form of calligraphy, demanding elegance as well as a perfect form to be effective.

Chinese poetry often expresses themes such as the desire for retreat from society, the love of nature, wine, and good company. Many poets are famous for their freedom from social convention and for their love of nature. The most famous of these is Li Po, who exhibits such freedom, and was ordained a Taoist priest at the T'ang court. His poems express his love of freedom from the mundane world, and of drinking under the moon—he is said to have drowned while trying to embrace the reflection of the moon in a lake.

Taoist practices continue to be central to the Chinese burial ceremony, which is the culture's most significant life-cycle ritual. The event involves the priest's reenactment of a cosmic drama of rescue and salvation for the souls of the deceased who face the infernal judiciary. Chinese theatre draws extensively on Taoist ritual, and many of its forms have evolved from it. Chinese theatrical works also often reenact stories containing Taoist elements and, prior to their performance, actors who represent certain deities undergo rituals of purification and abstinence which are similar to the ceremonies undertaken by priests before performing their rites.

Despite their frequent rivalry, Taoism provided a means of acculturation for Buddhism to East Asia, which traveled to China from India via the Silk Road at the beginning of the Common Era. Buddhism was first thought to be a foreign version of Taoism, and many Buddhist terms and ideas were translated—incorrectly—using Taoist terminology. This allowed for accommodation of Buddhism to the radically different Chinese context. Translators gradually became more knowledgeable and sophisticated, and Buddhism developed specifically Chinese forms. The most striking of these is the Ch'an (Zen) school, which has been described as a marriage between Buddhism and Taoism.

Finally, although Taoism did not fundamentally challenge the patriarchal structure of Chinese society, its emphasis on the female deviated from tradition. Taoist cloisters offered women an alternative to family life. Those who might become Taoist nuns included women who were unable to marry because of inauspicious horoscopes, those who were widowed or divorced, and unmarried girls who were permitted by male relatives to follow this vocation. In the T'ang dynasty, aristocratic women could be ordained before, after, or between marriages; two princesses were among the ordained. Women were often intermediaries with the divine and also played important roles as libationers in the Celestial Masters government. Female adepts are presumed to have an easier course to follow in internal alchemy and in creating an "embryo of immortality" (see p.91)—their bodies being already prepared for conception and gestation; in some texts, male adepts are given feminine behaviors (such as sitting before urinating) to follow in order to help them attain the Tao.

The Tao and Artistic Creation

66 It should be possible ... for the human spirit to express
the spirit of the universe through the brushwork without difficulty. For painting is only an art, yet it has the
power of creation of the universe itself. ... When the
artist is ready to start a picture, his mind can plan only
the general type of brushwork and composition. Yet as
the splash of ink descends upon the paper, guided by
the artist's spirit, it comes out in myriad forms entirely
beyond the original plan ... If the artist insists on
doing what he did yesterday, he cannot do it. Why?
Because when an artist insists on something, he is
already obstructing the free flow of the spirit. ... A
scholar painting starts out with nothing in his mind,
but when his spirit begins to move the brush, the
forms of objects present themselves on paper, for it
is the circumstance of a moment, totally unexpected,
and hard to explain in words. In a brief moment the
depths and heights appear, all well expressed by the
brushwork, and the disposition of different objects is
perfect, too, better even than the actual scenery. This
is because the grand idea [of the universe] has been
thereby expressed. 99

From *Chieh-chou Hsüeh Hua P'ien* [*The Art of Painting*], by Shen Tsung-ch'ien, translated by Lin Yutang in
The Chinese Theory of Art. New York: G.P. Putnam's Sons, 1967, p.204.

Commentary

Taoist ideas are integral to the Chinese arts and have had a profound influence on East Asian artistic traditions. The Taoist ideal of creative spontaneity has, in particular, helped to shape theory and practice in various art forms. Creative spontaneity involves the ability to draw upon one's personal resources while responding to a particular moment and circumstance. It is presumed that an artist has cultivated and nurtured their craft—but in creating art, knowledge and skill become experiential and intuitive, the unique possession of the artist and something that cannot be transmitted in words. This also describes the action of the Tao, which draws on limitless and formless content and possibility, and brings forth myriad creation.

Shen Tsun-ch'ien's words demonstrate a fundamentally Taoist attitude toward the theory of painting, whereby the art form is perceived, in essence, as an act of creation, beginning in the formlessness of the Tao, transforming in time and pattern into creation: what is captured is a universe in miniature, a microcosm. The artist creates this *wu-wei*, not forcing the brush, not thinking discursively, but moving with sensitivity in the moment. In this way, painting becomes a form of meditation, a means of discovering union with Tao, an accomplishment evident in the very best art.

TRANSLITERATIONS GLOSSARY

Modern China has ten main dialects, four of which collectively constitute Mandarin—the language of official China. In the 19th century the system most widely used to romanize Chinese written characters was known as Wade-Giles, but it was replaced by the People's Republic of China with a less complicated system of writing standard Chinese phonetically in a Latin script, known as Pinyin. This book uses Wade-Giles and the following list includes the main subjects with their Pinyin equivalents.

Persons and deities

Ch'ang-o / Chang E
Ch'iu Ch'ang-ch'un / Qiu Changchun
Ch'ü Yüan / Qu Yuan
Chang Lu / Zhang Lu
Chang Tao-ling / Zhang Daoling
Chen-wu / Zhenwu
Chuang-tzu / Zhuangzi
Chung-li Ch'üan / Zhongli Quan
Fan K'uan / Fan Kuan
Fu-hsing / Fuxing
Hsi Wang Mu / Xiwang mu
Huang-ti / Huangdi
Hun-tun / Hundun
K'ou Ch'ien-chih / Kou Qianzhi
Ko Hung / Ge Hong
Kuan-ti / Guandi
Kuan-yin / Guanyin
Lao-tzu / Laozi
Lieh-tzu / Liezi
Li Hung / Li Hong
Li Po / Li Bo
Lü Tung-pin / Lu Dongbin
Lu-hsing / Luxing
Ma-tzu / Mazu
Pi-hsia yüan-chün / Bixia yuanjun
San Kuan / San Guan
Shou-hsing / Shouxing
T'ai-i / Taiyi
T'ai-shang Lao-chün / Taishang Laojun
Tu Kuang-t'ing / Du Guangting
Wang Che / Wang Zhe
Wu Ch'eng-en / Wu Chengen
Yang Hsi / Yang Xi

Places

Peking / Beijing
Kuo-tien / Guodian
K'un-lun / Kunlun
Lung-hu Shan/ Longhu Shan
Ma-wang-tui / Mawangdui
P'eng-lai / Penglai
T'ai Shan / Tai Shan
Tun-huang / Dunhuang

Texts

Chuang-tzu / Zhuangzi
*Han Wu-ti nei-chuan / Han Wudi
    neizhuan*
Hsiang-erh / Xiang'er
Hua-hu ching / Huahu jing
Huai-nan-tzu / Huainanzi
I Ching / Yijing
Lieh-tzu / Liezi
Pao-p'u tzu / Bao Puzi
T'ai-p'ing ching / Taiping jing
Tao Te Ching / Daode Jing
Tao-tsang / Daozang
Wen-hsüan / Wenxuan

Events and practices

Ch'ing-ming / Qingming
chiao / jiao
Chia-tzu / jiazi
ch'i-kung / qigong
feng-shui
t'ai-chi ch'üan / taiji quan

Schools, sects, and movements

Ch'an / Chan
Ch'üan-chen / Quanzhen
Cheng-i / Zhengyi
Ling-pao / Lingbao
San-huang / Sanhuang
Shang-ch'ing / Shangqing

GENERAL BIBLIOGRAPHY

Baldrain, Farzeen., Lagerwey, John., Magee Boltz, Judith., and Barrett, T.H. "Taoism" in *The Encyclopedia of Religion* (ed. Mircea Eliade), Vol. 14., pp.288–332. New York: Macmillan, 1987.

Chan, Wing-tsit. *A Source Book in Chinese Philosophy*. Princeton: Princeton University Press, 1963.

De Bary, William Theodore., et al., eds. *Sources of Chinese Tradition*. Vols. 1 and 2, 2nd ed. New York: Columbia University Press, 1999.

Graham, A.C. *Chuang-tzu: The Inner Chapters*. London: Allen & Unwin, 1981.

——. *Disputers of the Tao*. LaSalle, Illinois: Open Court Publishing Company, 1989.

I Ching. Trans. by Richard Wilhelm, and from German to English by Cary F. Baynes. 3rd ed. Princeton: Princeton University Press, 1967.

Jordan, David. *Gods, Ghosts, and Ancestors: The Folk Religion of a Taiwanese Village*. Berkeley: University of California Press, 1972.

Kohn, Livia., ed. *The Daoist Handbook*. Leiden: Brill, 2000.

——. *The Taoist Experience*. Albany: State University of New York Press, 1993.

Lao-Tzu. *The Tao Te Ching*. Trans. by D.C. Lau. Baltimore: Penguin, 1963.

Lau, D.C. and Ames, Roger T. *Yuan Dao: Tracing Dao to its Source*. New York: Ballantine Books, 1998.

Maspero, Henri. *Taoism and Chinese Religion*. Trans. by Frank A. Kerman, Jr. Amherst: University of Massachusetts Press, 1981.

Overmyer, Daniel L. *Religions of China: The World as a Living System*. San Francisco: Harper & Row, 1986.

Overmyer, Daniel L.; Alvin P. Cohen; N.J. Girardot and Wing-tsit Chan. "Chinese Religions" in *The Encyclopedia of Religion* (ed. Mircea Eliade), Vol. 3., pp.257–323. New York: Macmillan, 1987.

Paper, Jordan. and Thompson, Laurence. *The Chinese Way in Religion*. 2nd ed. Belmont, California: Wadsworth, 1998.

Pas, Julien. *Historical Dictionary of Taoism*. Lanham, Maryland: The Scarecrow Press, Inc., 1998.

Robinet, Isabelle. *Taoism: Growth of a Religion*. Trans. Phyllis Brooks. Palo Alto, California: Stanford University Press, 1997.

Saso, Michael. *Blue Dragon, White Tiger: Taoist Rites of Passage*. Washington, D.C.: The Taoist Center, 1990.

Stepanchuk, Carol. and Wong, Charles. *Mooncakes and Hungry Ghosts: Festivals of China*. San Francisco: China Books and Periodicals, 1991.

Thompson, Laurence. *Chinese Religion: An Introduction*. 5th ed. Belmont, California: Wadsworth, 1998.

Welch, Holmes. *Tao: The Parting of the Way*. Boston: Beacon Press, 1966.

Wong, Eva., trans. *Seven Taoist Masters*. Boston: Shambhala Press, 1990.

Wu, Ch'eng-en. *Monkey*. Trans. by Arthur Waley. New York: Grove Press, 1943.

INDEX

ACKNOWLEDGMENTS AND PICTURE CREDITS

Unless cited otherwise here, text extracts are out of copyright or the product of the author's own translation. The following sources have kindly given their permission.

Sacred Space, p.70: From *Hsing-shih yin-yuan chuan* [*Xingshi yinyuan zhuan*] by Hsi Chou Sheng, translated by Glen Dudbridge in Susan Naquin and Chün-fang Yü, eds. *Pilgrims and Sacred Sites in China.* University of California Press, 1992, p.46.

Sacred Time, p.82: From the *Heart-Mirror of Mnemonics and Explanations from Writings on the Elixir,* translated by Nathan Sivin in N. Sivin, "Chinese Alchemy and the Manipulation of Time" in N Sivin, ed., *Science and Technology in East Asia.* New York: Science History Publications, 1977, p.112.

From *Arcane Teachings on the Ninefold Cyclically Transformed Gold Elixir,* translated by Nathan Sivin in N. Sivin, "Chinese Alchemy and the Manipulation of Time" in N. Sivin, ed., *Science and Technology in East Asia.* New York: Science History Publications, 1977, p.115.

Society and Religion, p.104: From *Chieh-chou Hsüeh Hua P'ien* by Shen Tsung-ch'ien, translated by Lin Yutang in *The Chinese Theory of Art.* New York: G.P. Putnam's Sons, 1967, p.204.

The publisher would like to thank the following people, museums, and photographic libraries for permission to reproduce their material. Every care has been taken to trace copyright holders. However, if we have omitted anyone we apologize, and will, if informed, make corrections in any future edition.

Page 2 Magnum Photos/Fred Mayer; 7 Bridgeman Art Library, London/Oriental Museum, Durham University; 12 Art Archive, London/British Museum, London; 18 Bridgeman Art Library, London/Oriental Museum, Durham University; 22 Réunion des Musées Nationaux/Musée Guimet, Paris/Thierry Ollivier; 26 British Museum, London; 32 Nelson-Atkins Museum of Art, Kansas City. Purchase Nelson Trust #48–17/Robert Newcombe; 37 AKG London/Bibliothèque Nationale, Paris; 42 Corbis/Lindsay Hebberd; 47 Bridgeman Art Library, London/Oriental Museum, Durham University; 52 Getty Images/Stone/Paul Harris; 58 Bridgeman Art Library, London/Oriental Museum, Durham University; 62 Werner Forman Archive, London; 66 Getty Images/Stone/Keren Su; 72 Panos Pictures, London/Jean Leo Dugast; 77 British Library, London; 84 Art Archive, London/British Library, London; 89 Corbis/Michael Yamashita; 96 Corbis/Carl & Ann Purcell; 100 Magnum Photos/Fred Mayer.